HOW TO USE THIS BOOK

Congratulations on buying this workbook! It will help you master the hiragana script - the basic script that is used in Japanese writing and an absolute necessity for studying Japanese language.

This workbook consists of 3 chapters:

1. Hiragana training course

This workbook is built around a 10-day intensive training course. Each day you will be introduced to 5 hiragana characters and offered ample space for writing practice. After you've finished writing characters on their own you will have an opportunity to write Japanese words that consist of characters that you have learned.

The volume of writing practice presumes that you will practice at least 60 minutes per day. If that time is not enough for you to finish the day's work, don't be discouraged! Take your time!

2. Cut-out hiragana flash cards

These pages are designed to be cut out and cut into smaller cards. The cards contain a hiragana character on one side and its romaji reading on the other. Flash cards will help you remember hiragana characters better!

3. Hiragana chart

Cut out this page and hang it on the wall where you'll be able to see it often.

勉強しよう!
[Benkyou shiyou!] — Let's study!

We are happily accepting feedback regarding this workbook at:
lilas.publishing@ya.ru

Lilas Lingvo Team

TABLE OF CONTENTS

The basics of Japanese writing 1

Day 1: Hiragana vowels...3

Day 2: Hiragana K-column..11

Day 3: Hiragana S-column..21

Day 4: Hiragana T-column..31

Day 5: Hiragana N-column..41

Day 6: Hiragana H-column..51

Day 7: Hiragana M-column..61

Day 8: Hiragana R-column..71

Day 9: Hiragana Y-column and digraphs..81

Day 10: Hiragana W-column and 'N' character 89

Cut-out Hiragana Flash Cards 97

Hiragana chart..109

THE BASICS OF JAPANESE WRITING

Written Japanese uses 3 different scripts: **hiragana, katakana and kanji**.

Hiragana is the basic Japanese alphabet. Contrary to the English alphabet each hiragana character represents only one syllable sound. So every time you see a specific character you know that it will always sound the same way. Here is a greeting written in hiragana:

こんにちは

[konnichiwa] - Hello! / Good afternoon!

Katakana is the second script used in Japanese. Each katakana character represents the same syllable as its hiragana counterpart. However it is written differently and it's used mostly for foreign words. Here is a word written in katakana:

アメリカ

[amerika] - America

Hiragana and katakana together are called 'kana'.

Kanji is the third script used in Japanese. Kanji characters do not represent syllables but rather words or concepts. Unlike hiragana and katakana there are thousands of kanji characters. Plus kanji characters often have different meanings and readings that depend on the context in which the character is used. It is important to learn kanji characters because they are essential in understanding the Japanese. Here's a phrase written with use of kanji:

お名前は何ですか

[o namae wa nan desu ka] - What is your name?

Notice that hiragana characters are used to spell out the reading of kanji characters. They are placed above or beside a kanji and written smaller. This use of hiragana is called 'furigana'.

In this workbook we will cover the hiragana script!

あ、い、う、え、お

DAY 1: HIRAGANA VOWELS

HIRAGANA VOWELS
あ [a], い [i], う [u], え [e], お [o]

Let's start learning hiragana. Hiragana is the most common of the three Japanese scripts. It is used to write functional words like grammatical particles. They can also be found at the end of adjectives and verbs. There are also words that are commonly written in hiragana rather than kanji. Here's an example of a Japanese sentence with hiragana (written in black):

[nihongo de hanashimashou] Let's talk in Japanese.

There are 46 hiragana characters. They are commonly arranged in this order:

HIRAGANA CHART

Let's start with the first column that contains symbols あ [a], い [i], う [u], え [e] and お [o]. These five characters are the five vowel sounds in Japanese. The rest of the characters are made up of the consonant sound and one of these vowel sounds except for the ん character.

To remember this character, notice that it has a letter 'A' hidden inside it.

[a]

Practice writing this character:

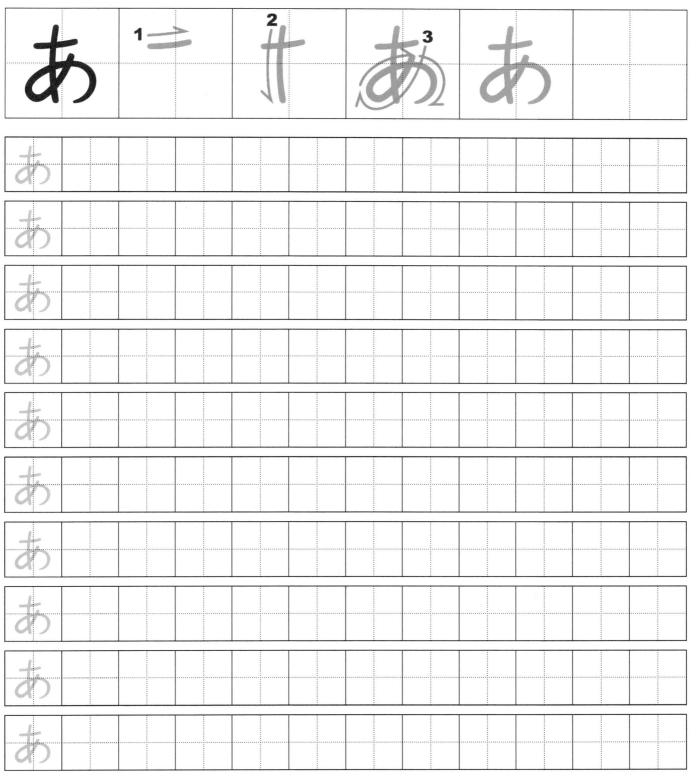

[i]

To remember this character, imagine it as two 'i's written side by side.

Practice writing this character:

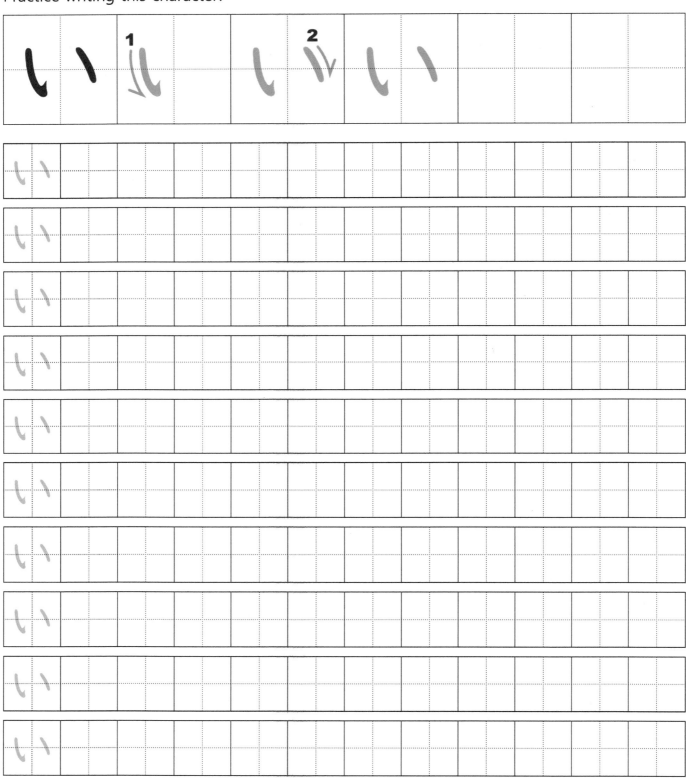

To remember this character, notice that it has an '<u>U</u>' turned on its side hidden in it.

[u]

Practice writing this character:

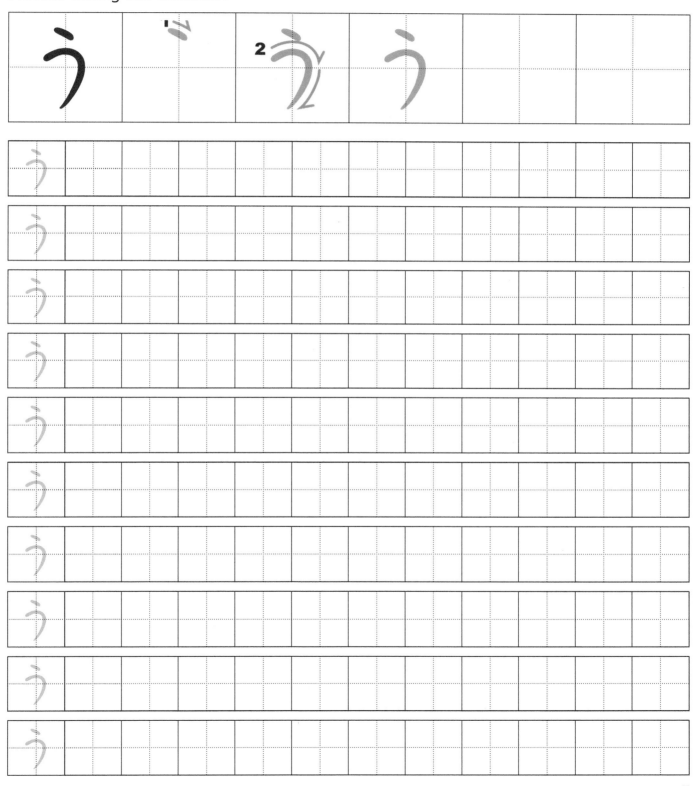

 **[e]**

 To remember this character, think of it like of <u>e</u>xotic bird sitting on its <u>e</u>gg.

Practice writing this character:

To remember this character, imagine it as an UF**O** landed on a <u>lawn</u>.

お
[o]

Practice writing this character:

WORD WRITING PRACTICE

Now let's revise the first five hiragana characters that we've learnt by writing some words with them!

あ あ [aa] — Ah! Oh!

あう [au] — to meet, to see

あおい [aoi] — blue

あい [ai] — love

うお [uo] — fish

いい [ii] — good

いう [iu] — to say

いえ [ie] — house

おおい [ooi] — many

か、き、く、け、こ

DAY 2: HIRAGANA K-COLUMN

HIRAGANA K-COLUMN

か [ka], き [ki], く [ku], け [ke], こ [ko]

Today you will learn 5 new characters and 10 new sounds. How is that?

Most of hiragana characters have a second reading when they have a mark that looks like a quotation mark at the upper right corner. It is called 'dakuten' or 'tenten'.

が

'Dakuten' makes the consonant of the syllable voiced. So, か [ka] with the 'dakuten' - が - will be pronounced as [ga].

You may wonder how to discern between the 'dakuten' and quotation marks? In Japanese corner brackets called 'kagikakko' are used instead of quotation marks to avoid confusion.

「ゴジラ」

[gojira] - "Godzilla"

Just like quotation marks corner brackets can be single (see above) or double. Double corner brackets are called 'nijuu kagikakko'. They are used to mark quotes within quotes: 「...『...』...」 as well as to mark book titles (Japanese does not have italic type, and does not use sloping type for this purpose). They are also sometimes used in fiction to denote text that is heard through a telephone or other device.

はやてさん、「今日は『ゴジラ』を見てみよう!」とのこと。

[Hayate-san, ˋkyou wa "Gojira" o mite miyou!' To no koto.]

Hayate-san said: 'Let's watch "Godzilla" today!'

And now let's proceed to learning new hiragana characters of the K-column!

To remember this character, imagine it as a blade <u>cut</u>ting a stick.

 **[ga]**

 **[ka]**

Practice writing this character:

[ki] **[gi]**

To remember this character, imagine it as a <u>key</u>.

Practice writing this character:

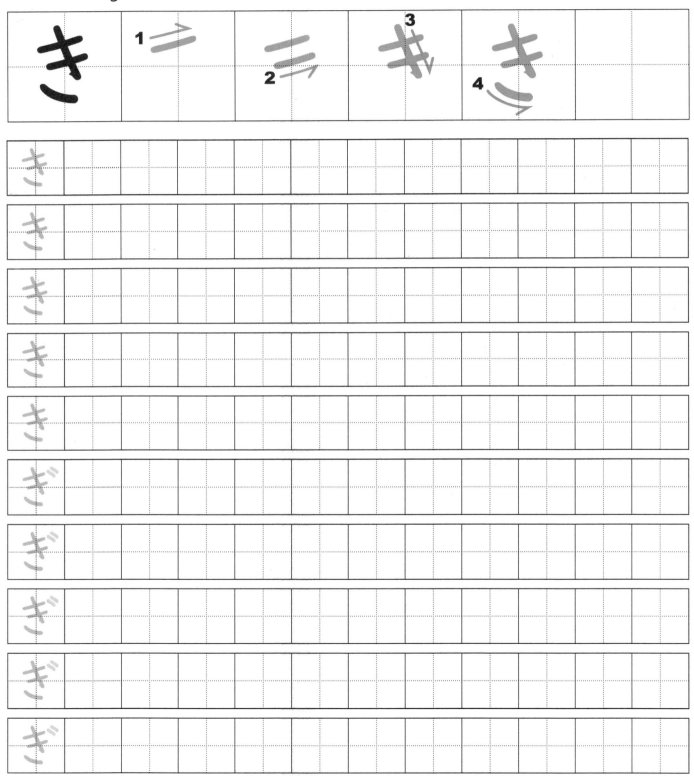

To remember this character, imagine it as a <u>cuckoo</u>'s beak.

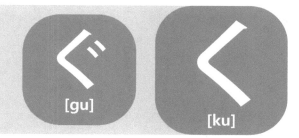

[gu]

[ku]

Practice writing this character:

[ke] **[ge]**

To remember this character, imagine it as a <u>keg</u>.

Practice writing this character:

To remember this character, imagine it as two <u>koi</u> fish.

[go]

[ko]

Practice writing this character:

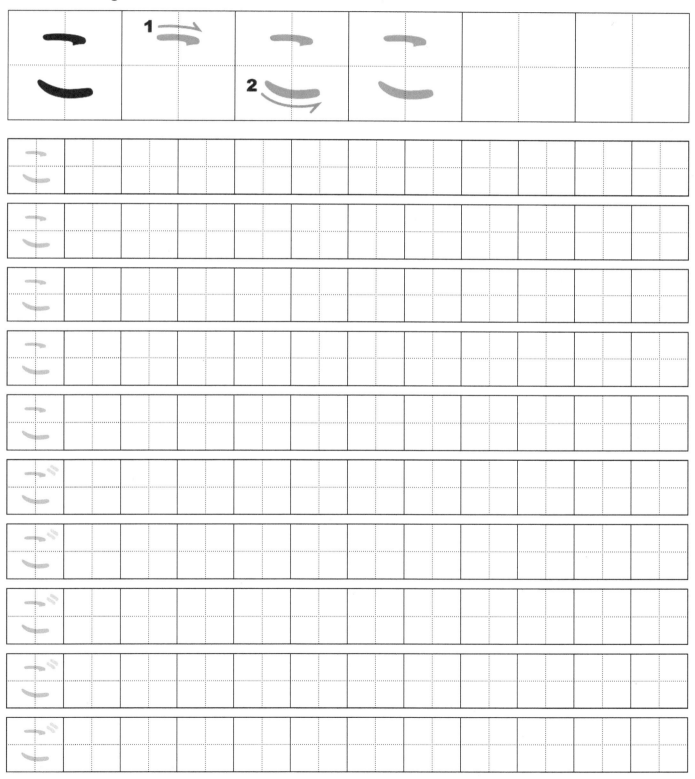

WORD WRITING PRACTICE

Let's revise the characters that we've learned and write some words with them!

あかい [akai] — red

あき [aki] — autumn

あく [aku] — to open

いかが [ikaga] — how, in what way

いく [iku] — to go

いけ [ike] — pond

えいが [eiga] — movie, film

えいご [eigo] — English language

えき [eki] — station

おおきい [ookii] — big

かお [kao] — face, person

おく [oku] — to put, to place

がいこく [gaikoku] — foreign country

かう [kau] — to buy

かお [kao] — face, person

かぎ [kagi] — keys

かく [kaku] — to write

ごご [gogo] — afternoon, p.m.

きく [kiku] — to listen

こえ [koe] — voice

けいかく keikaku — plan

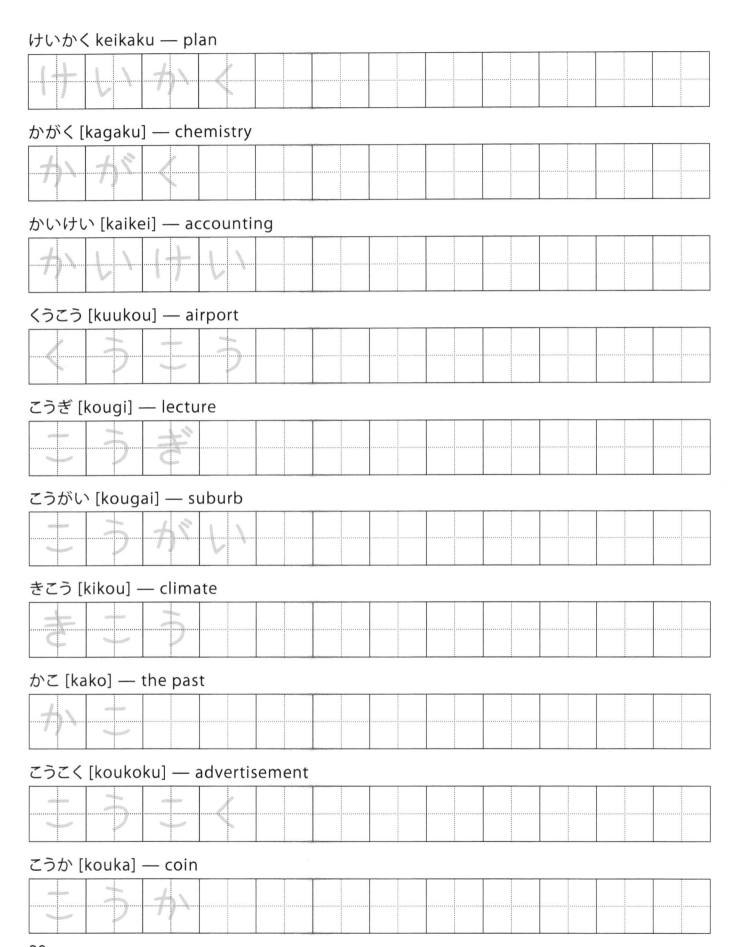

けい　かく

かがく [kagaku] — chemistry

かが　く

かいけい [kaikei] — accounting

かい　けい

くうこう [kuukou] — airport

くう　こう

こうぎ [kougi] — lecture

こう　ぎ

こうがい [kougai] — suburb

こう　がい

きこう [kikou] — climate

きこ　う

かこ [kako] — the past

かこ

こうこく [koukoku] — advertisement

こう　こく

こうか [kouka] — coin

こう　か

さ、し、す、せ、そ

DAY 3: HIRAGANA S-COLUMN

HIRAGANA S-COLUMN
さ [sa], し [shi], す [su], せ [se], そ [so]

Today you will learn 5 new characters and again 10 new sounds.

To remember this character, imagine it as a <u>sa</u>d face.

Practice writing this character:

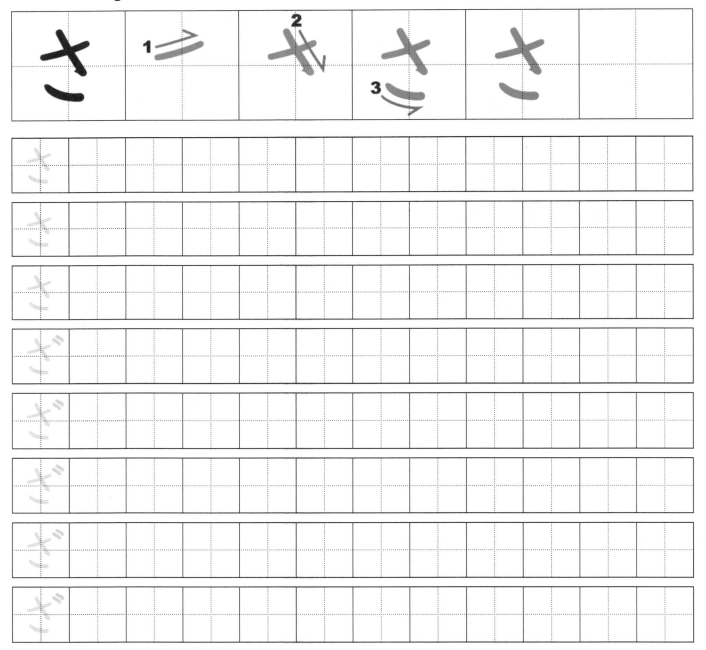

To remember this character, imagine it as a fi<u>sh</u>ing hook.

じ [ji]　し [shi]

Practice writing this character:

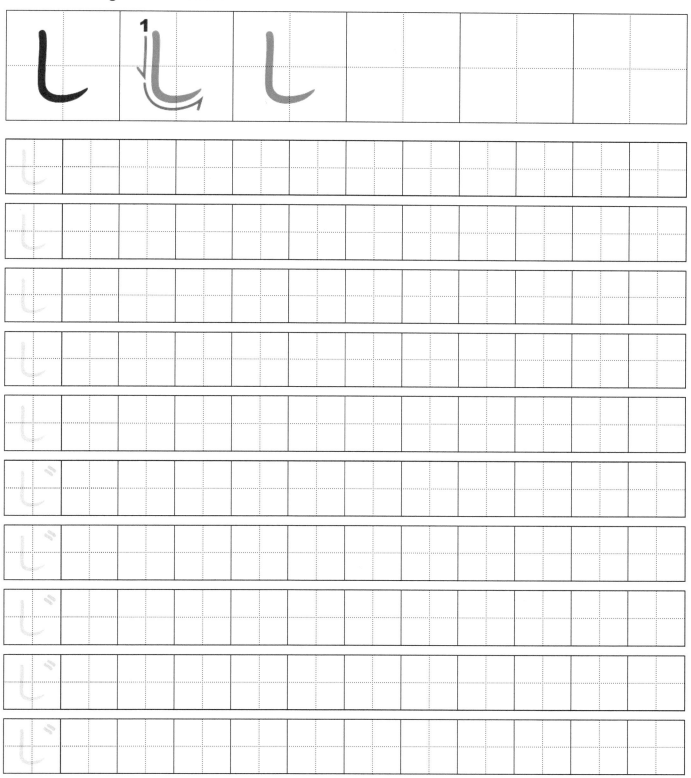

[su]　　**[zu]**

To remember this character, imagine it as a <u>soup</u> laddle in a pot.

Practice writing this character:

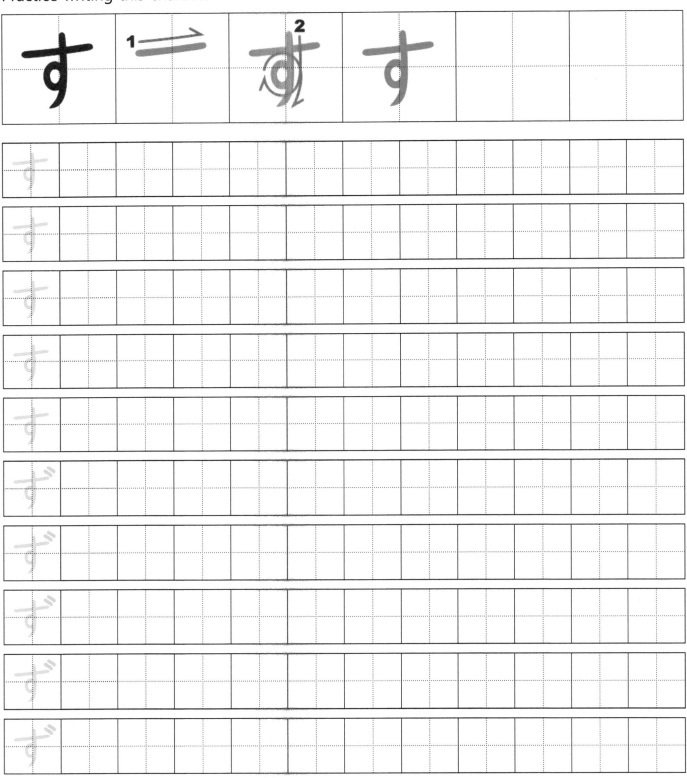

24

Remember this character by imagining it as a <u>security</u> guard in a hat.

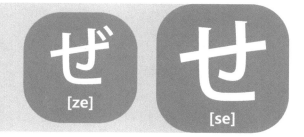
[ze]

[se]

Practice writing this character:

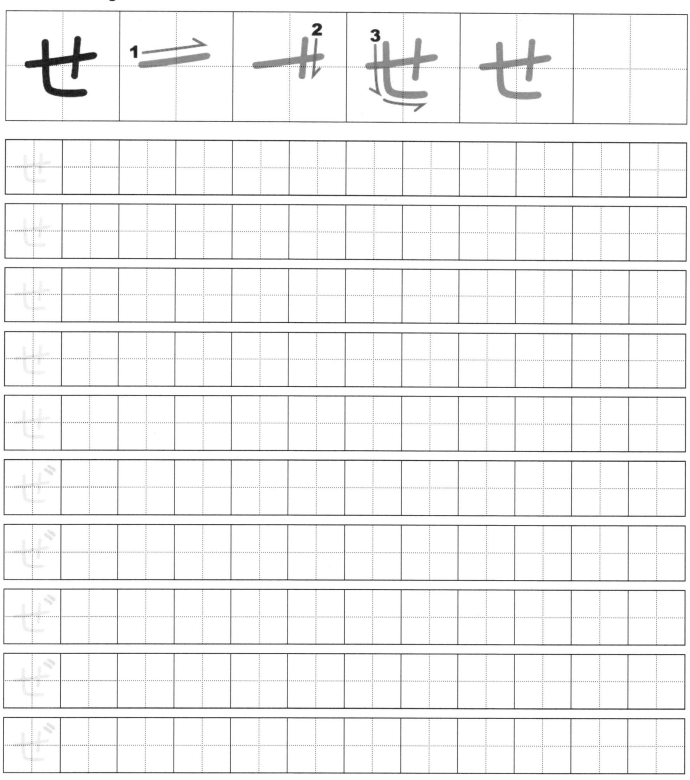

[so] **[zo]**

Remember this character by imagining it as a zigzag <u>sew</u>ing stich.

Practice writing this character:

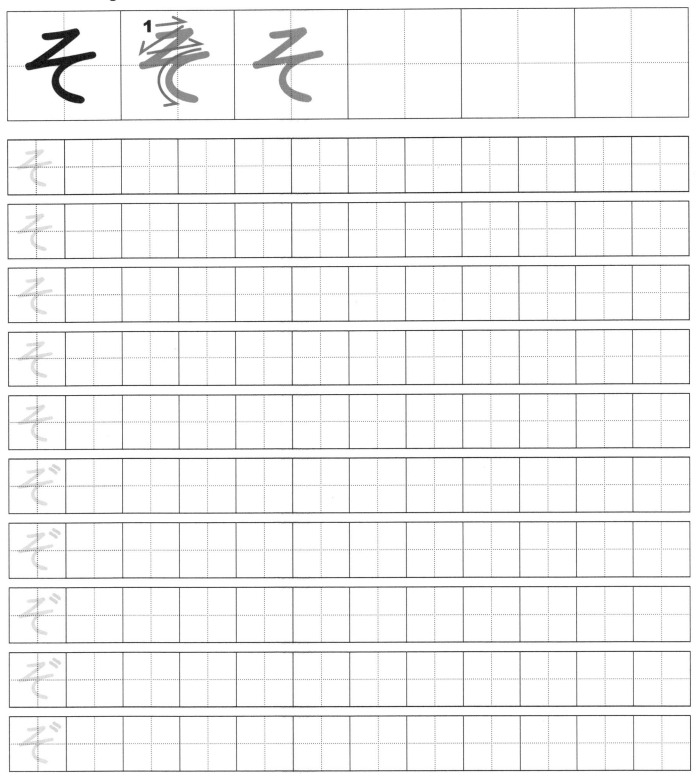

WORD WRITING PRACTICE

Let's revise the characters that we've learned and write some words with them!

かさ [kasa] — umbrella

おす [osu] — to push

あさ [asa] — morning

あし [ashi] — foot, leg

あそこ [asoko] — over there

いす [isu] — chair

いそがしい [isogashii] — busy

うすい [usui] — thin, weak

おいしい [oishii] — tasty, delicious

おおぜい [oozei] — a lot (of people)

おおぜい

おじ [oji] — uncle

おじ

おかし [okashi] — sweets

おかし

おそい [osoi] — late, slow

おそい

おさけ [osake] — sake, alcohol

おさけ

かえす [kaesu] — to return something

かえす

がくせい [gakusei] — student

がくせい

かす [kasu] — to lend

かす

かぜ [kaze] — wind, breeze

かぜ

かぞく [kazoku] — family

かぞく

けさ [kesa] — this morning

けす [kesu] — to erase, to turn off

さき [saki] — future, former, previous

さく [saku] — to bloom

しお [shio] — salt

しずか [shizuka] — quiet, peaceful

すき [suki] — like

すこし [sukoshi] — little, few

すずしい [suzushii] — cool, refreshing

そうじ [souji] — cleaning, sweeping

うそ [uso] — lie, untruth

きそ [kiso] — foundation, basis

くうそう [kuusou] — daydream; fantasy

そうこ [souko] — warehouse

せい [sei] — surname

すうがく [suugaku] — mathematics

すいえい [suiei] — swimming

さか [saka] — slope; hill

えさ [esa] — pet food

た、ち、つ、て、と

DAY 4: HIRAGANA T-COLUMN

HIRAGANA T-COLUMN

た [ta], ち [ti], つ [tsu], て [te], と [to]

Today you'll learn 5 characters, 10 sounds and a new character function.

Imagine this character as an English syllable 'ta' to remember it better.

Practice writing this character:

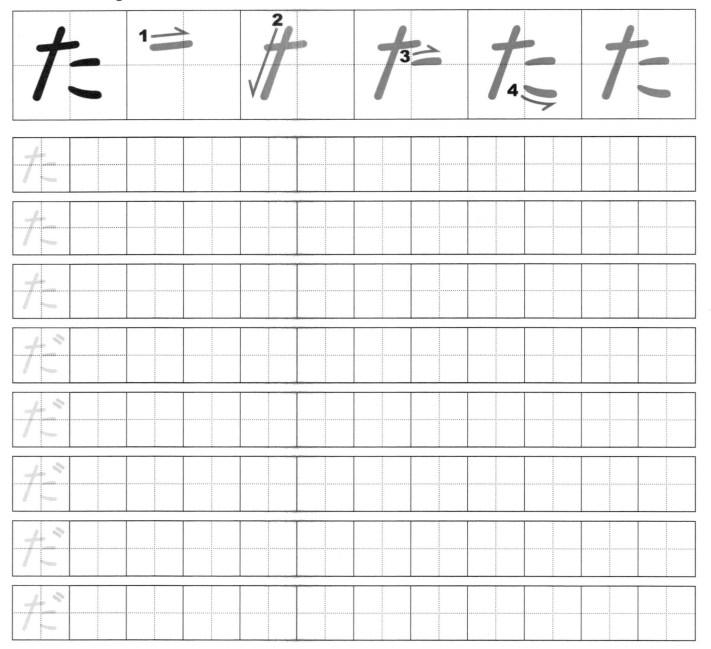

Imagine this character as a face with a forced smile when someone says: "Cheese!"

ぢ [dji]   ち [chi]

Practice writing this character:

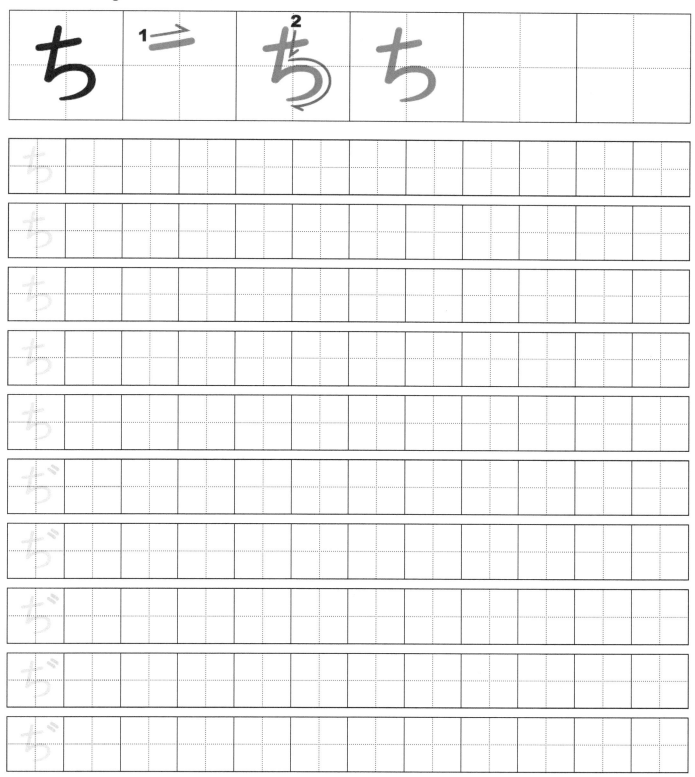

33

This character is very easy to remember. It looks like a <u>tsu</u>nami wave!

This character has a smaller version called 'chiisai tsu' (small 'tsu'). It is used to prolong the consonant that it's followed by. For example:

かっこいい
[kakkoii] - cool

がっこう
[gakkou] - school

かった
[katta] - bought

Practice writing this character:

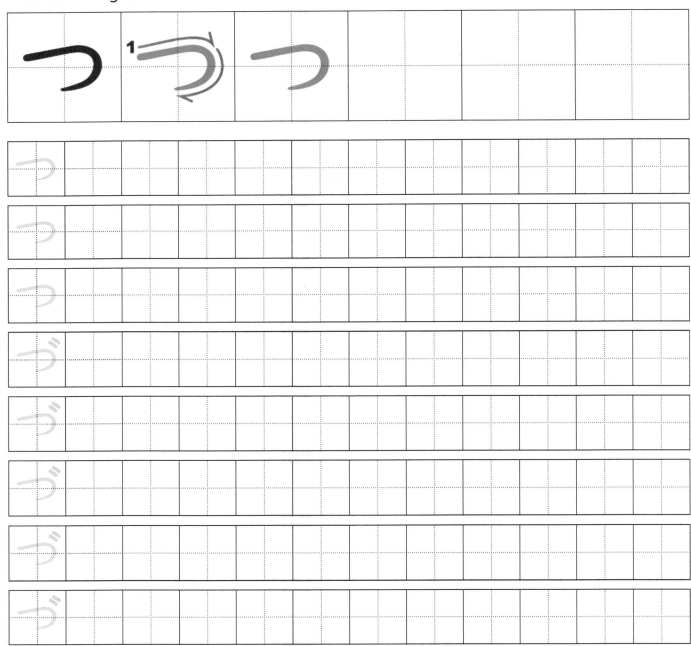

To remember this character, think of it as a dog's <u>tail</u>.

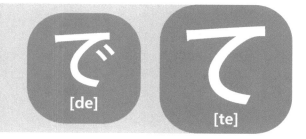
[de] [te]

Practice writing this character:

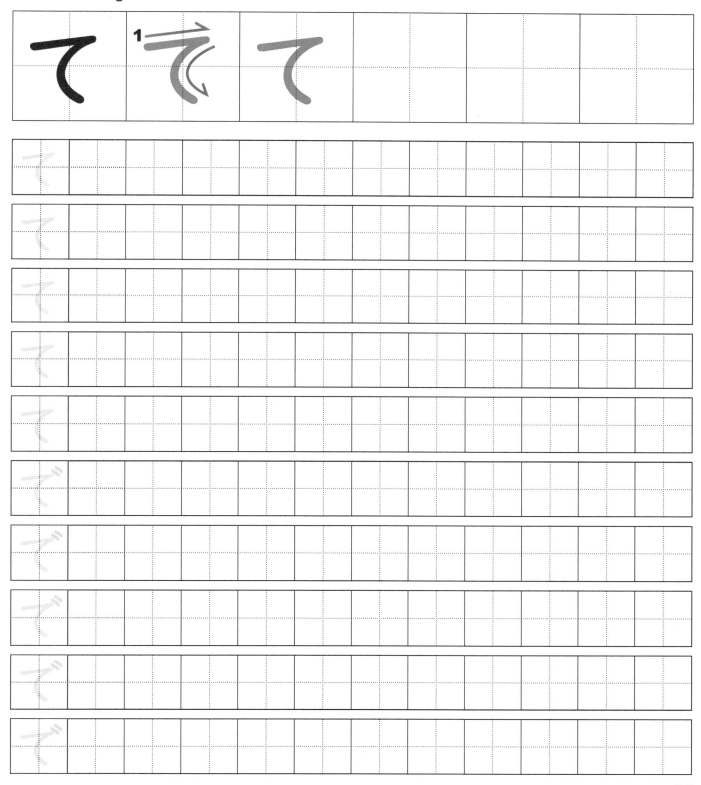

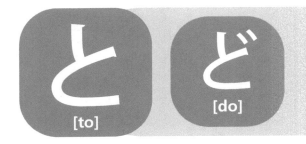

[to] [do]

Imagine this character as a <u>tornado</u> to remember it better.

Practice writing this character:

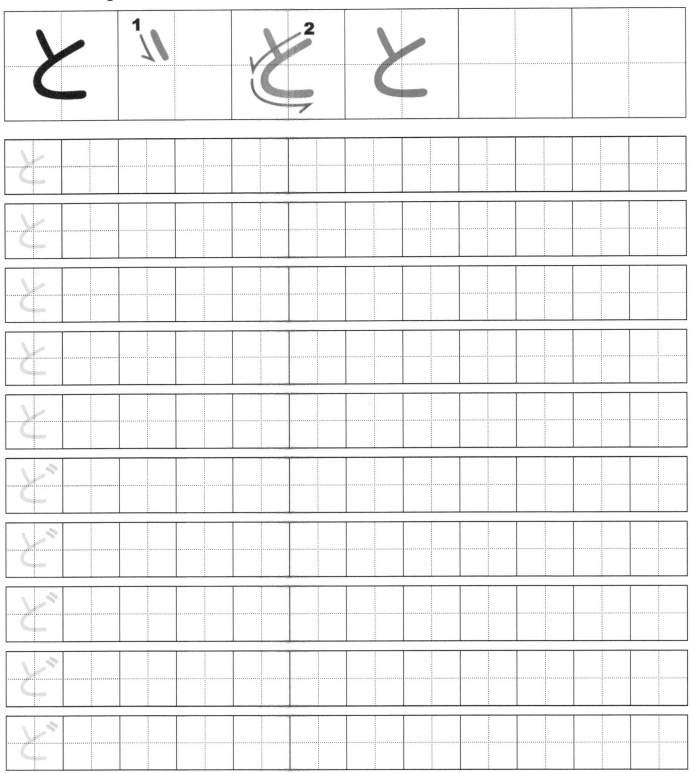

WORD WRITING PRACTICE

Let's revise the characters that we've learned and write some words with them!

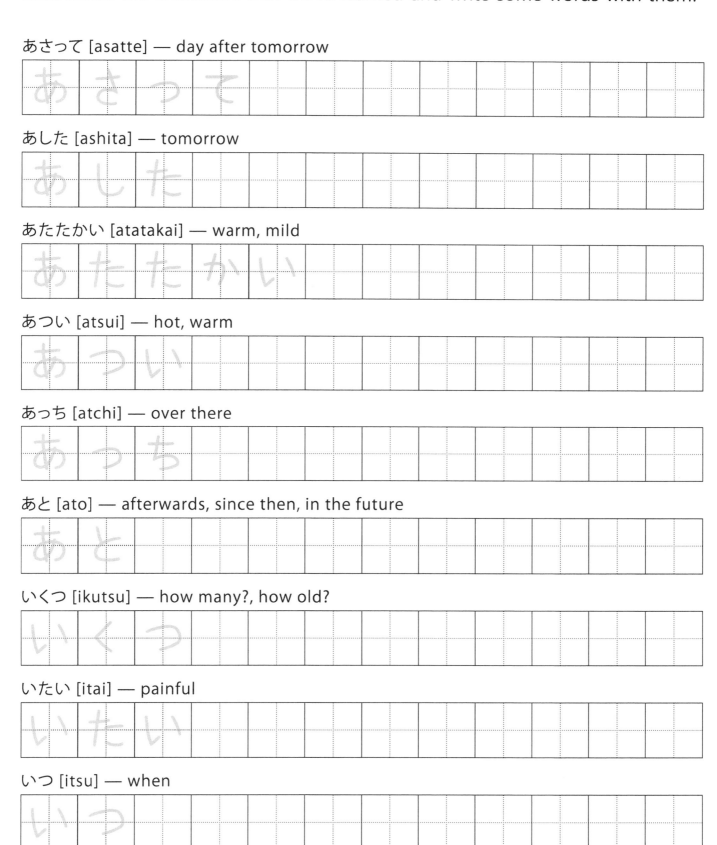

あさって [asatte] — day after tomorrow

あした [ashita] — tomorrow

あたたかい [atatakai] — warm, mild

あつい [atsui] — hot, warm

あっち [atchi] — over there

あと [ato] — afterwards, since then, in the future

いくつ [ikutsu] — how many?, how old?

いたい [itai] — painful

いつ [itsu] — when

いつか [itsuka] — five days, the fifth day (of the month)

いつか

うた [uta] — song

うた

うち [uchi] — house (one's own)

うち

おとこ [otoko] — man

おとこ

おとうと [otouto] — younger brother

おとうと

おととい [ototoi] — day before yesterday

おととい

おととし [ototoshi] — year before last

おととし

かた [kata] — person

かた

がっこう [gakkou] — school

がっこう

かてい [katei] — home, household

かてい

かど [kado] — corner

きた [kita] — north

きって [kitte] — stamp (postage)

ください [kudasai] — (with te-form verb) please do for me

くち [kuchi] — mouth

くつ [kutsu] — shoes, footwear

くつした [kutsushita] — socks

けっこう [kekkou] — quite

ことし [kotoshi] — this year

さとう [satou] — sugar

した [shita] — under, below, beneath

せいと [seito] — pupil

そうして [soushite] — and, like that

そと [soto] — outside, exterior

だいがく [daigaku] — university

だいすき [daisuki] — very likeable, like very much

たいせつ [taisetsu] — important

たかい [takai] — tall, high, expensive

ちいさい [chiisai] — small, little

ちかい [chikai] — near, close by, short

な、に、ぬ、ね、の

DAY 5: HIRAGANA N-COLUMN

HIRAGANA N-COLUMN

な [na], に [ni], ぬ [nu], ね [ne], の [no]

Today you'll learn 5 characters and 5 new sounds. 'Dakuten' is not used with N-characters as they are already voiced.

 **[na]**

💡 Imagine this character as a <u>n</u>un praying in front of a cross to remember it better.

Practice writing this character:

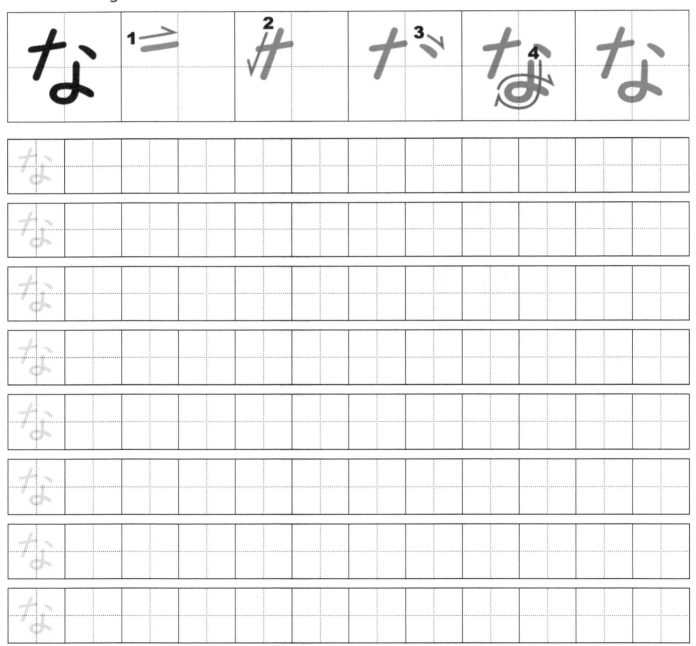

Remember this character by imagining it as a <u>knee</u>.

[ni]

Practice writing this character:

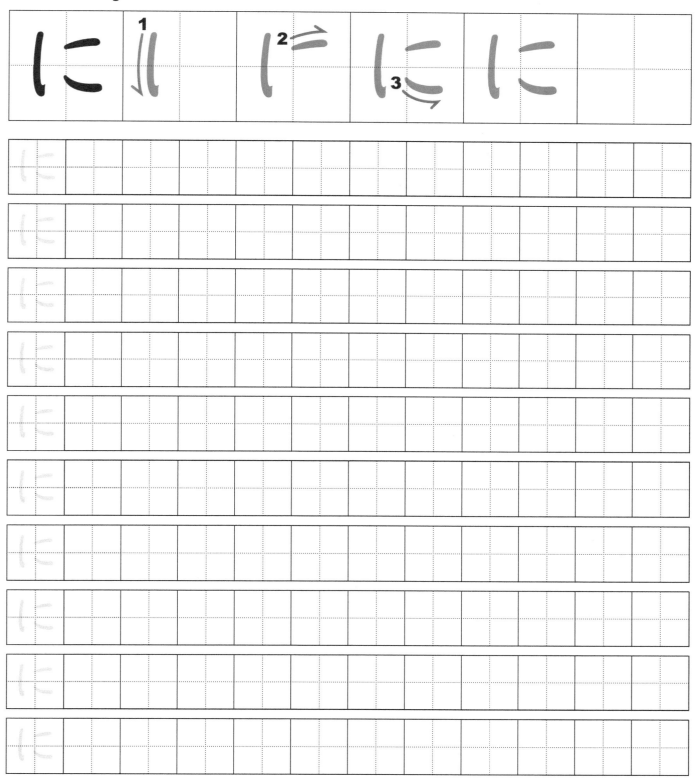

 [nu]

 Imagine this character as a bowl of <u>noo</u>dles with chop sticks to remember it better.

Practice writing this character:

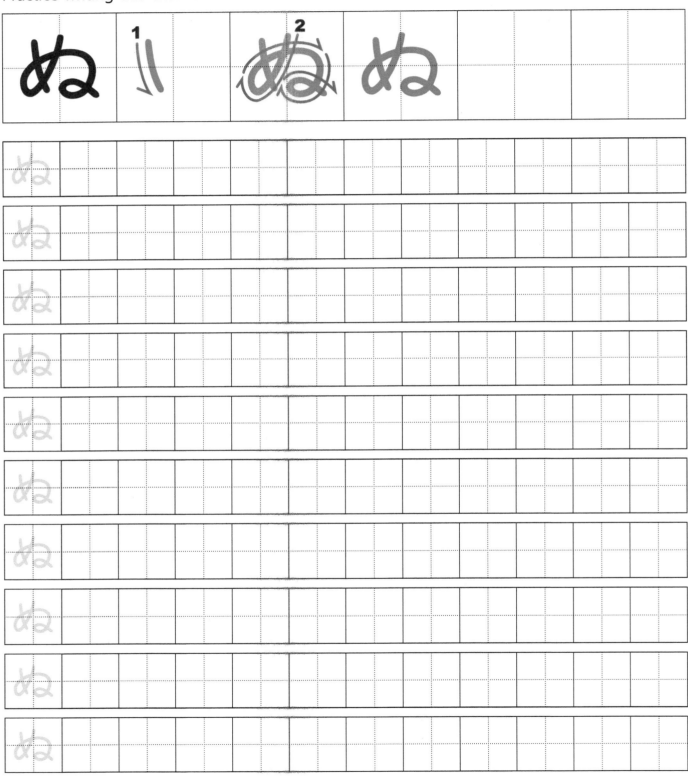

Think of this character as a s<u>n</u>ail hiding behind a <u>n</u>ail to remember it better.

[ne]

Practice writing this character:

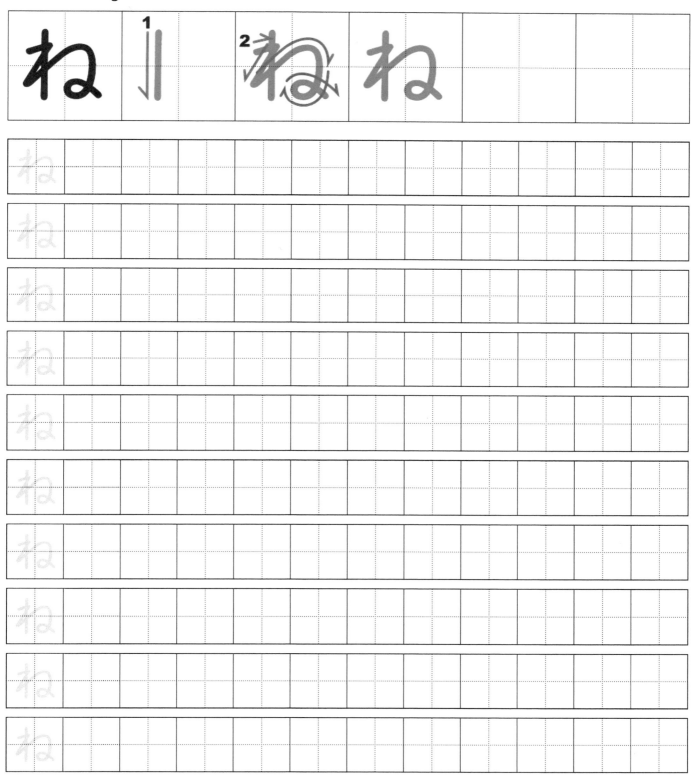

 [no]

 This character is easy to remember as it looks like a <u>no</u>-sign.

Practice writing this character:

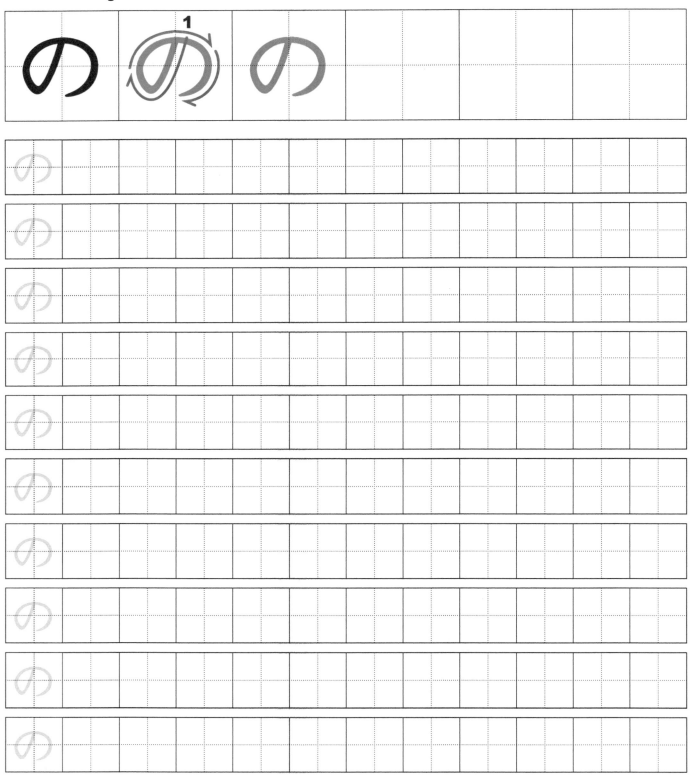

WORD WRITING PRACTICE

Let's revise the characters that we've learned and write some words with them!

あなた [anata] — you

あに [ani] — older brother

あね [ane] — older sister

あの [ano] — there, over there

おかね [okane] — money

おとこのこ [otokonoko] — boy

おとな [otona] — adult

おなか [onaka] — stomach

おなじ [onaji] — same, identical, similar

かたかな [katakana] — katakana

きたない [kitanai] — dirty, messy

きのう [kinou] — yesterday

くに [kuni] — country

この [kono] — this

さかな [sakana] — fish

すくない [sukunai] — a few, scarce

その [sono] — that

たのしい [tanoshii] — enjoyable, fun

どなた [donata] — who

48

どの [dono] — which

なか [naka] — inside, middle, among

ながい [nagai] — long

なく [naku] — to sing (bird), to make sound (animal)

なくす [nakusu] — to lose something

ねこ [neko] — cat

なつ [natsu] — summer

にく [niku] — meat

にし [nishi] — west

ぬぐ [nugu] — to take off clothes

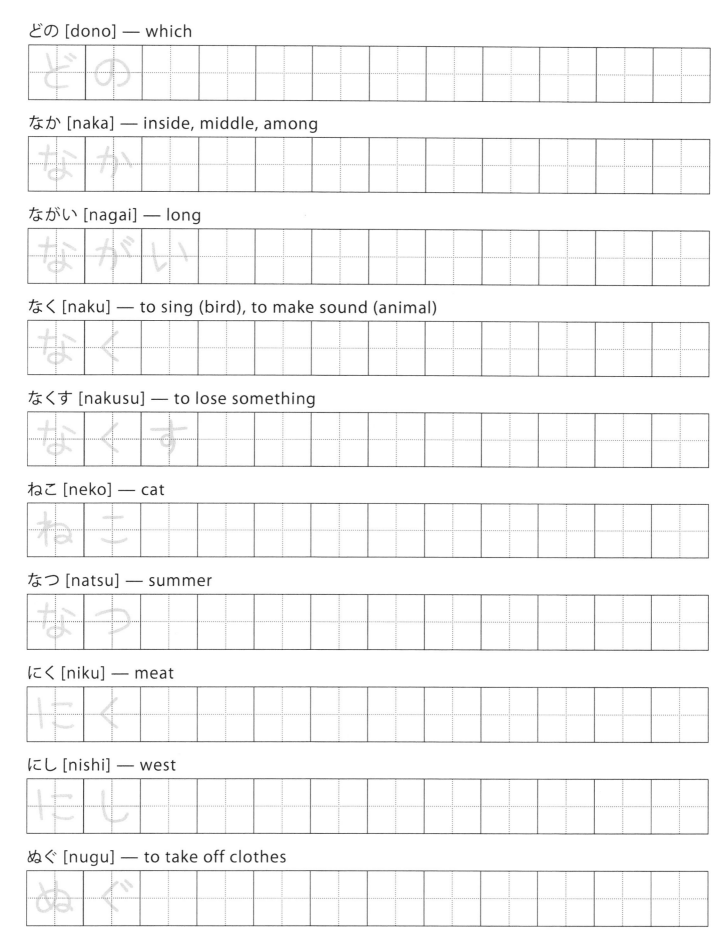

かきね [kakine] — hedge; fence

かきね

ねじ [neji] — screw

ねじ

ねがい [negai] — desire; hope

ねがい

おに [oni] — ogre; demon

おに

なに [nani] — what

なに

なぜ [naze] — why

なぜ

にがい [nigai] — bitter

にがい

おおいに [ooini] — very; much; greatly

おおいに

あいにく [ainiku] — unfortunately

あいにく

のうか [nouka] — farmer

のうか

は、ひ、ふ、へ、ほ

DAY 6: HIRAGANA H-COLUMN

HIRAGANA H-COLUMN

は [ha], ひ [hi], ふ [fu], へ [he], ほ [ho]

Today you'll learn 5 characters and 16 new sounds.

H-characters can be modified with the 'dakuten'. With the 'dakuten' they will start with 'b'. For example:

は　　ば

[ha]　　[ba]

H-characters can also be modified with another mark - the 'handakuten' or 'maru'. With this mark H-characters will start with 'p'. For example:

は　　ぱ

[ha]　　[pa]

The first character in the H-column - は [ha] - is very popular as it is used to mark the topic of the sentence. The word or phrase that comes before は [ha] is the topic of the sentience.

Remember! When は is used as topic-marking particle it is pronounced as [wa]. For example:

はこはおおきいです。

[hako wa ookii desu] - The box is big.

ははははながすき。

[haha wa hana ga suki] - Mother likes flowers.

This last sentence is actually a good example of why kanji are important. If written only in hiragana it will be confusing even for native speakers. With kanji it will be much more readable:

母は花が好き。

[haha wa hana ga suki] - Mother likes flowers.

[pa]

[ba]

[ha]

Practice writing this character:

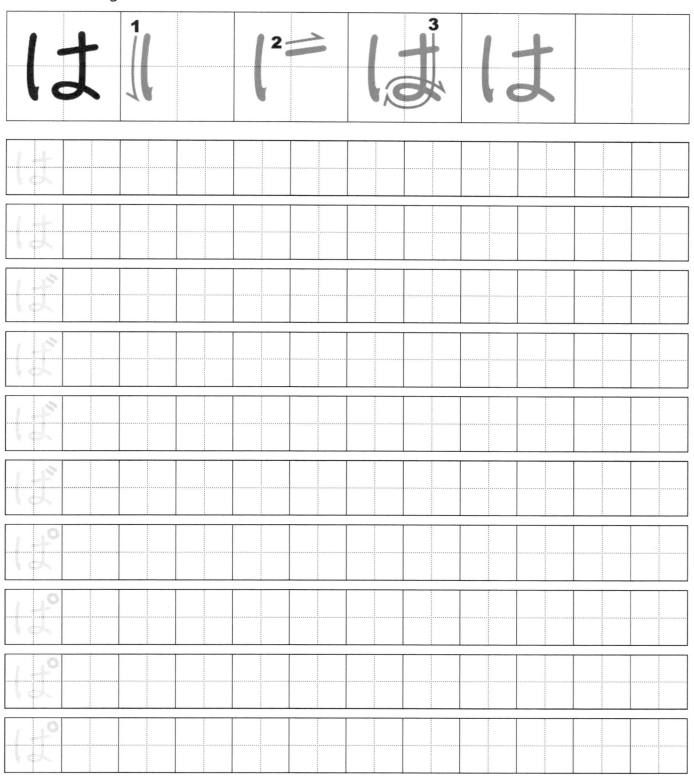

This character looks like a smile saying: "Hi-hi-hi!"

Practice writing this character:

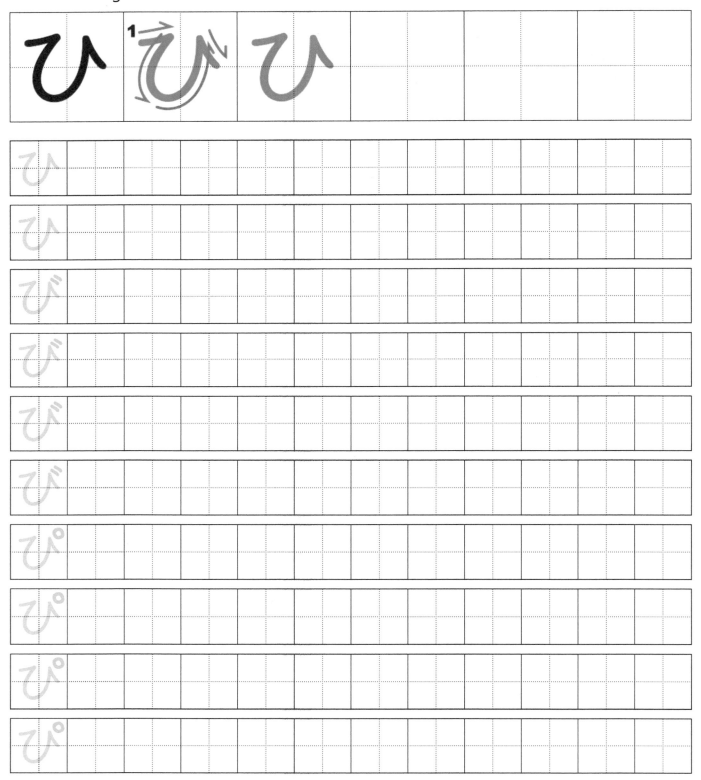

This character is pronounced as [fu] and looks like Mount Fuji.

 [pu]

 [bu]

 [fu]

Practice writing this character:

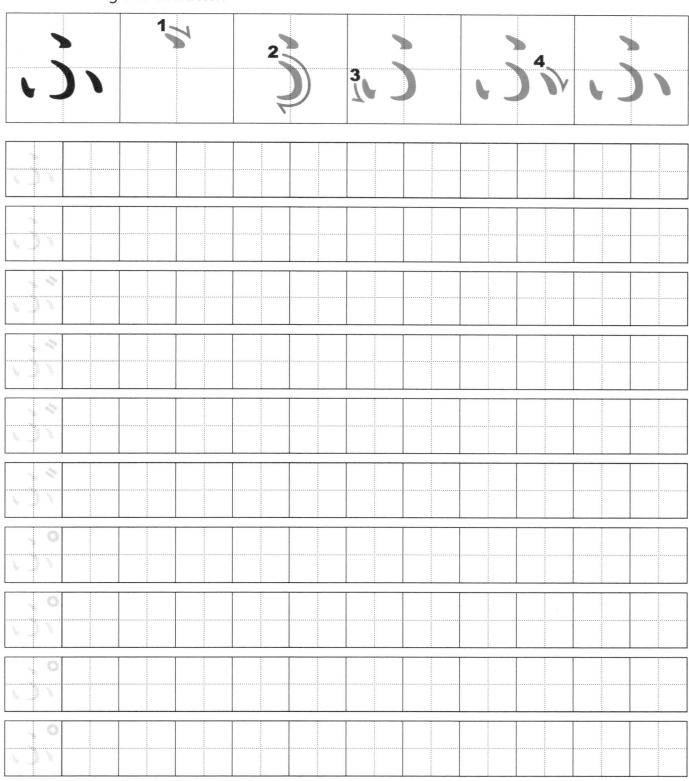

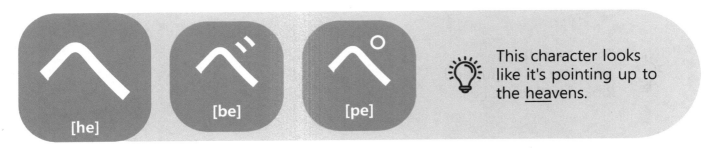

[he]   [be]   [pe]

This character looks like it's pointing up to the <u>heavens</u>.

Practice writing this character:

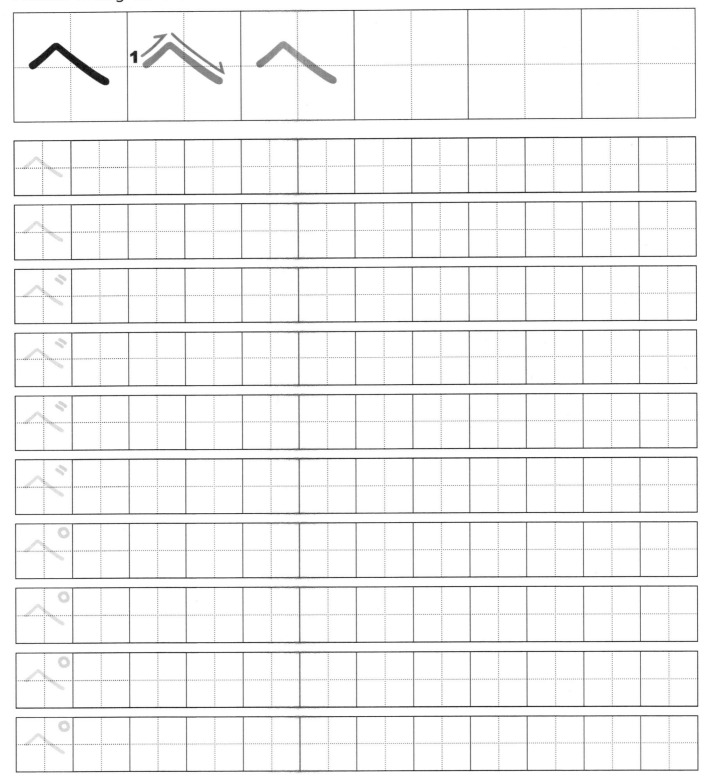

Remember that は only has <u>half</u> the horizontal lines and ほ has <u>whole</u> lot of them.

[po]

[bo]

[ho]

Practice writing this character:

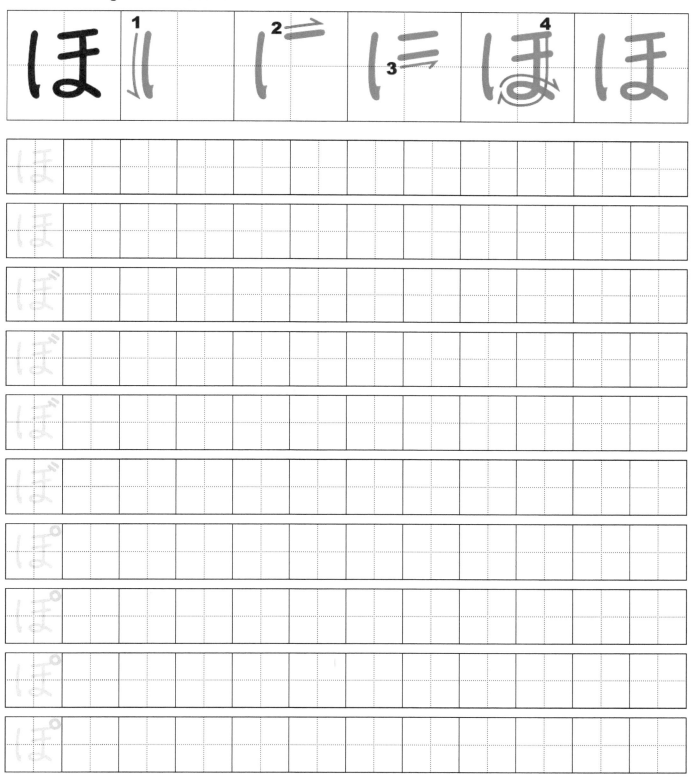

WORD WRITING PRACTICE

Let's revise the characters that we've learned and write some words with them!

は [ha] — tooth

は													

はい [hai] — yes

はい													

あぶない [abunai] — dangerous, critical, watch out!

あぶない										

おば [oba] — aunt

おば												

ことば [kotoba] — word

ことば											

そば [soba] — near, close, beside

そば											

たばこ [tabako] — tobacco, cigarettes

たばこ											

はいざら [haizara] — ashtray

はいざら										

はがき [hagaki] — postcard

はがき											

はく [haku] — to wear

はこ [hako] — box

はし [hashi] — bridge or chopsticks

はな [hana] — nose or flower

はは [haha] — (own) mother

はなし [hanashi] — talk, story

はなす [hanasu] — to speak

ひく [hiku] — to pull or to play (guitar, piano)

ひくい [hikui] — short, low

ひこうき [hikouki] — airplane

ひと [hito] — man, person

ひと

ふうとう [fuutou] — envelope

ふうとう

ふく [fuku] — to blow (wind)

ふく

ぶたにく [butaniku] — pork

ぶたにく

ふとい [futoi] — fat, thick

ふとい

へた [heta] — unskilled, poor

へた

ぼうし [boushi] — hat

ぼうし

ほか [hoka] — other place, the rest

ほか

ほしい [hoshii] — want, in need, desire

ほしい

ほそい [hosoi] — thin, slender, fine

ほそい

ま、み、む、め、も

DAY 7: HIRAGANA M-COLUMN

HIRAGANA M-COLUMN

ま [ma], み [mi], む [mu], め [me], も [mo]

Today you'll learn 5 new characters and 5 new sounds.

 Try imagining this character as a <u>ma</u>sked face to remember it better.

Practice writing this character:

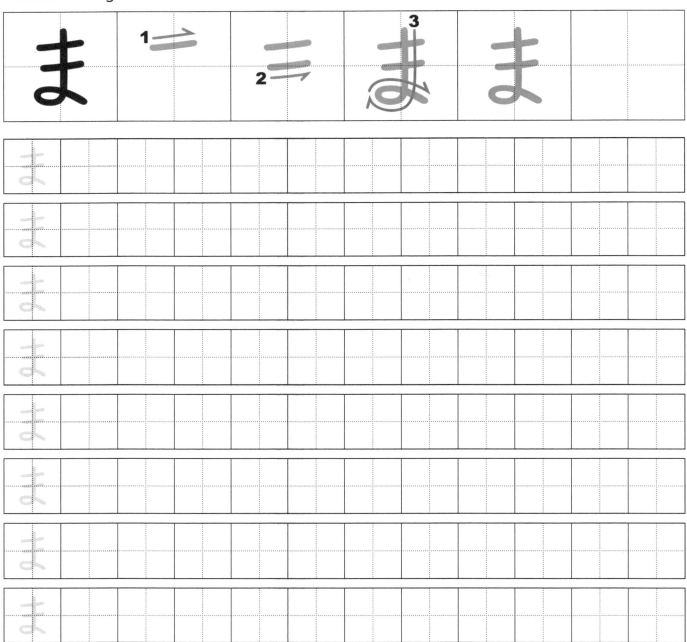

Remember this character by imagining it as a musical note '<u>mi</u>'.

[mi]

Practice writing this character:

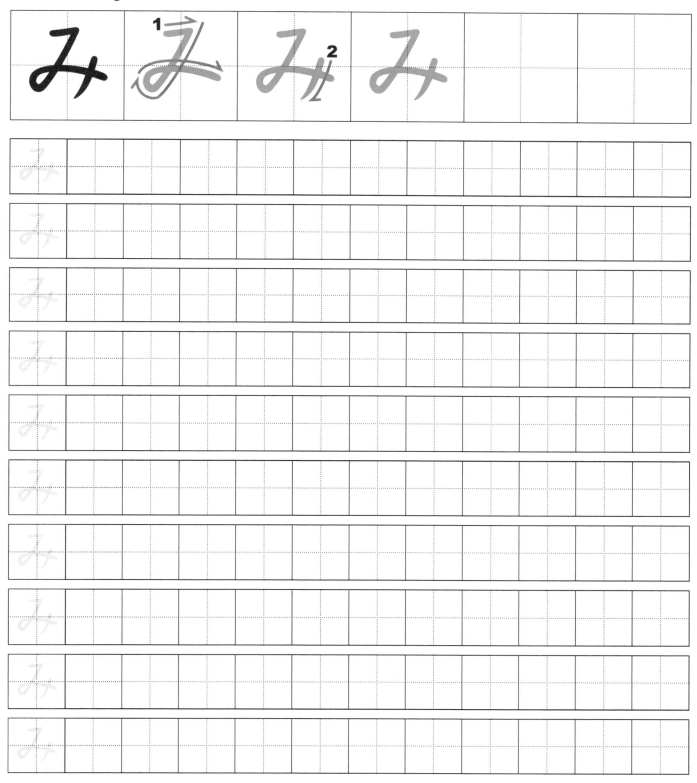

[mu]

 Imagine this character as a cow wagging its tail.
And what do cows say? "Moo!"

Practice writing this character:

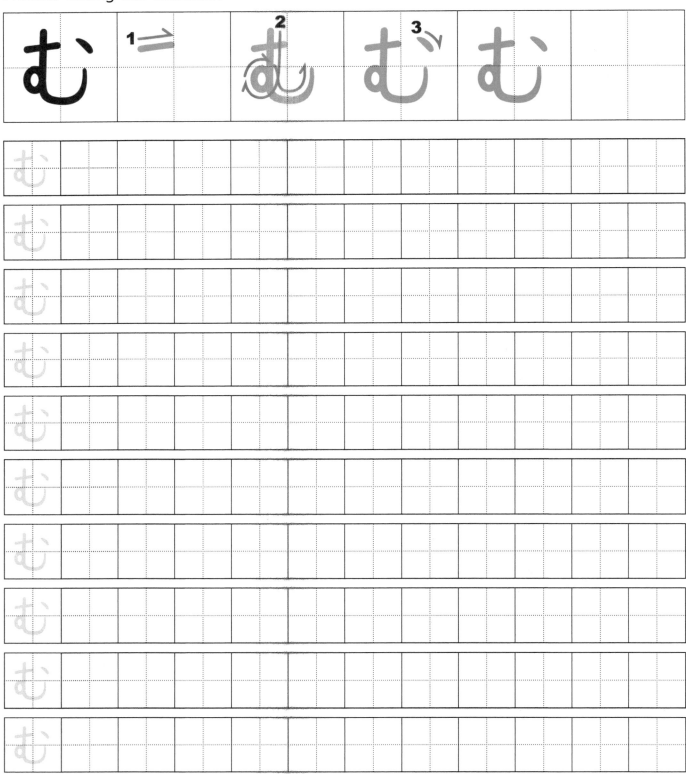

め [Me] means 'eye' in Japanese and this character looks like an eye.

[me]

Practice writing this character:

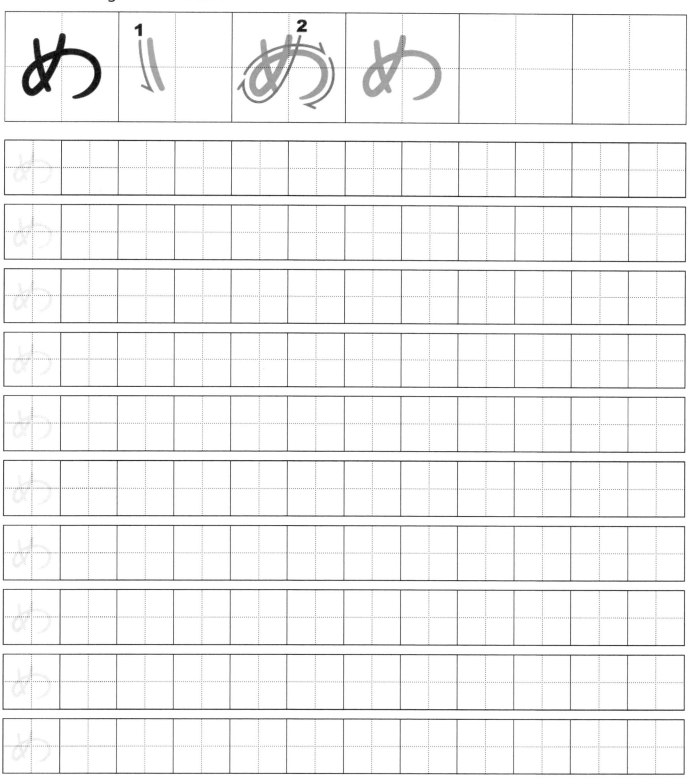

[mo]

 This character looks like a し - <u>fish</u>ing hook - with horizontal lines. You can catch <u>more</u> fish if you add <u>more</u> worms to your hook.

Practice writing this character:

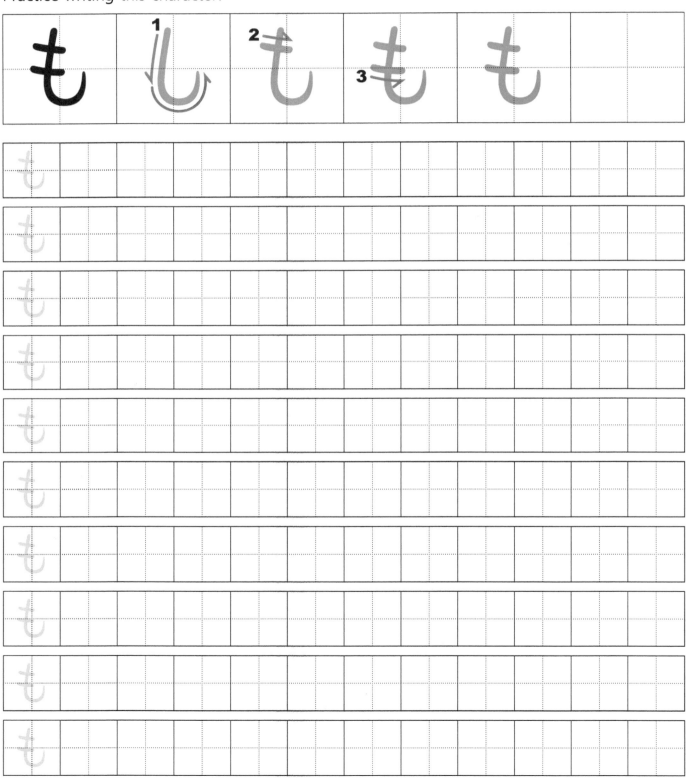

WORD WRITING PRACTICE

Let's revise the characters that we've learned and write some words with them!

まち [machi] — town, city

まっすぐ [massugu] — straight, ahead, direct

まど [mado] — window

うみ [umi] — sea, beach

かみ [kami] — paper

てがみ [tegami] — letter

のみもの [nomimono] — drink, beverage

みがく [migaku] — to brush (teeth)

みじかい [mijikai] — short

みず [mizu] — water

みち [michi] — road, street

みなみ [minami] — south

みみ [mimi] — ear

さむい [samui] — cold (weather etc.)

すむ [sumu] — to reside, to live in

たのむ [tanomu] — to request, to ask

のむ [nomu] — to drink

むずかしい [muzukashii] — difficult

あめ [ame] — rain

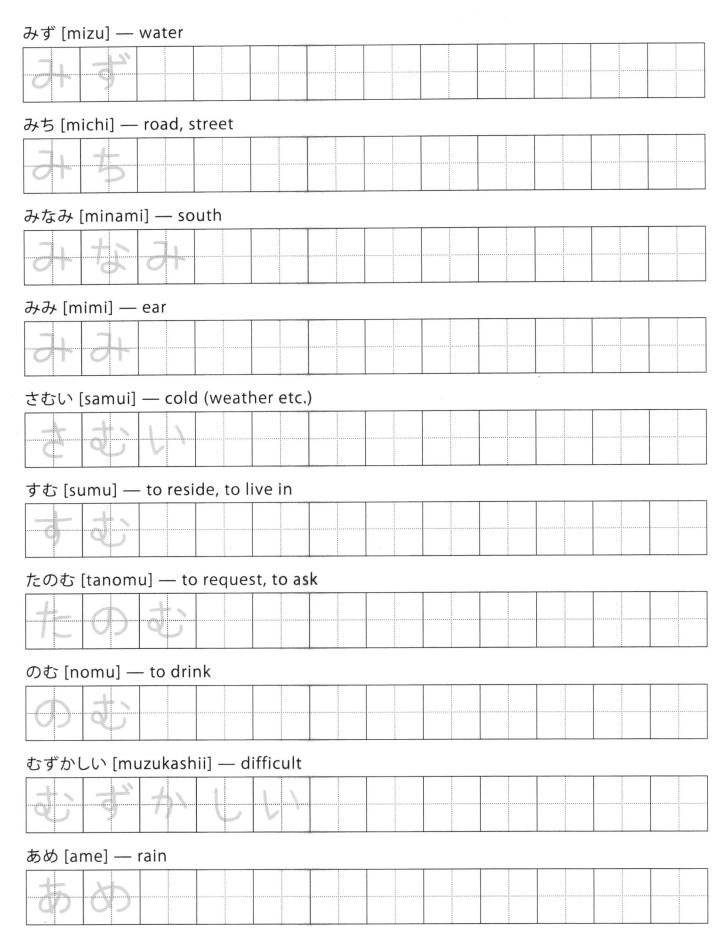

つめたい [tsumetai] — cold (to touch)

つめたい

はじめ [hajime] — beginning, start

はじめ

めがね [megane] — eye glasses

めがね

いつも [itsumo] — always, all the time

いつも

いもうと [imouto] — younger sister

いもうと

おもい [omoi] — heavy

おもい

こども [kodomo] — question

こども

たてもの [tatemono] — child

たてもの

たべもの [tabemono] — food

たべもの

ともだち [tomodachi] — friend

ともだち

あたま [atama] — head

むすこ [musuko] — son

むね [mune] — chest

せつめい [setsumei] — explanation

せいめい [seimei] — life; existence

めし [meshi] — cooked rice

ゆうめい [yuumei] — famous

めいし [meishi] — business card

なまえ [namae] — name

まいにち [mainichi] — every day

70

ら、り、る、れ、ろ

DAY 8: HIRAGANA R-COLUMN

HIRAGANA R-COLUMN

ら [ra], り [ri], る [ru], れ [re], ろ [ro]

Today you'll learn 5 new characters and 5 new sounds.

 Try imagining this character as a <u>r</u>abbit sitting on its hind legs.

Practice writing this character:

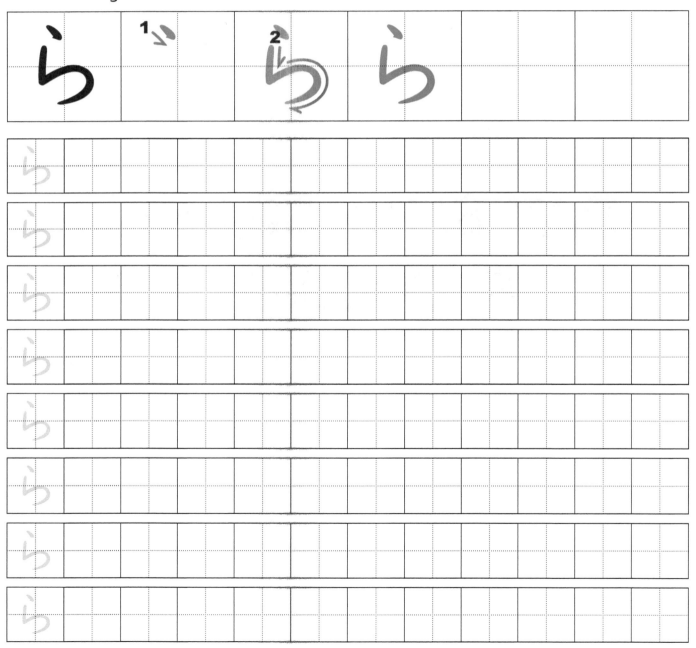

Imagine this character as a flowing <u>ri</u>ver with <u>ree</u>ds growing along its banks.

[ri]

Practice writing this character:

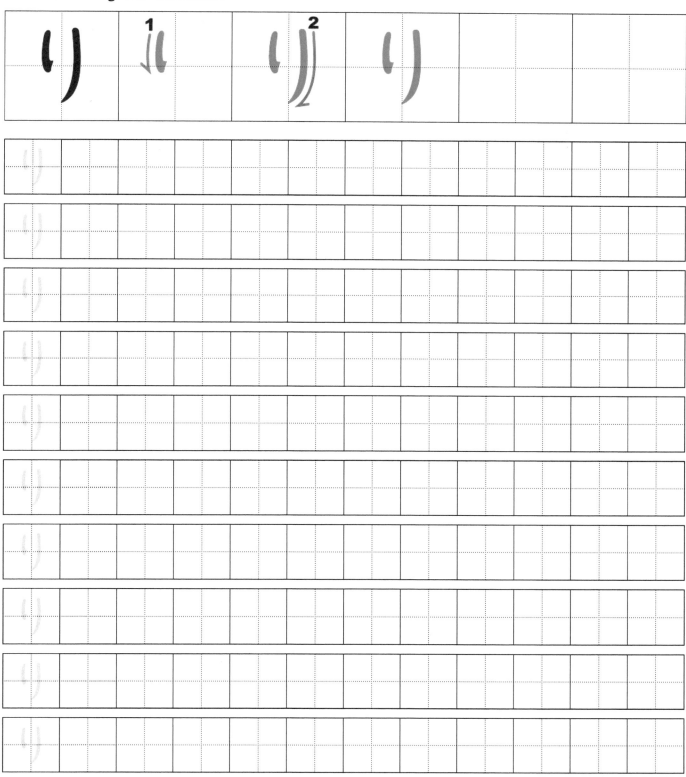

 To remember this character imagine it as a hand holding a <u>ruby</u>.

Practice writing this character:

Remember this character by imagining it as a <u>re</u>indeer looking up.

Practice writing this character:

 This character looks a lot like る [ru] - a hand holding a ruby. But ろ has no ruby, so it got <u>robbed</u>.

[ro]

Practice writing this character:

WORD WRITING PRACTICE

Let's revise the characters that we've learned and write some words with them!

くらい [kurai] — dark, gloomy

く ら い

そら [sora] — sky

そ ら

それから [sorekara] — and then, after that

そ れ か ら

ならう [narau] — to learn

な ら う

はたらく [hataraku] — to work

は た ら く

ひらがな [hiragana] — hiragana

ひ ら が な

むら [mura] — village

む ら

りっぱ [rippa] — splendid, fine

り っ ぱ

あまり [amari] — not very, not much

あ ま り

いりぐち [iriguchi] — entrance, gate

いりぐち

かりる [kariru] — to borrow

かりる

くすり [kusuri] — medicine

くすり

となり [tonari] — next to, next door to

となり

とり [tori] — bird

とり

とりにく [toriniku] — chicken meat

とりにく

ひだり [hidari] — left side

ひだり

いれる [ireru] — to put in

いれる

うまれる [umareru] — to be born

うまれる

きれい [kirei] — pretty, clean, tidy

きれい

つかれる [tsukareru] — to get tired, to tire

いろいろ [iroiro] — various

うしろ [ushiro] — behind, rear

おふろ [ofuro] — bath

おもしろい [omoshiroi] — interesting, amusing

きいろい [kiiroi] — yellow

くろい [kuroi] — black

しろい [shiroi] — white

だいどころ [daidokoro] — kitchen

ひろい [hiroi] — spacious, wide

ちから [chikara] — force; strength

ち か ら

さら [sara] — plate; dish

さ ら

しんらい [shinrai] — reliance; trust

し ん ら い

みどり [midori] — green

み ど り

くもり [kumori] — cloudiness

く も り

もり [mori] — forest

も り

れきし [rekishi] — history

れ き し

めいれい [meirei] — order; command

め い れ い

だれ [dare] — who

だ れ

こころ [kokoro] — mind; heart

こ こ ろ

や、ゆ、よ

DAY 9: HIRAGANA Y-COLUMN AND DIGRAPHS

HIRAGANA Y-COLUMN AND DIGRAPHS

や [ya], ゆ [yu], よ [yo]

Today you'll learn 3 new characters and a whole 33 new sounds!

 **[ya]**

 Remember this character by imagining it as a <u>ya</u>k's head with two horns.

Practice writing this character:

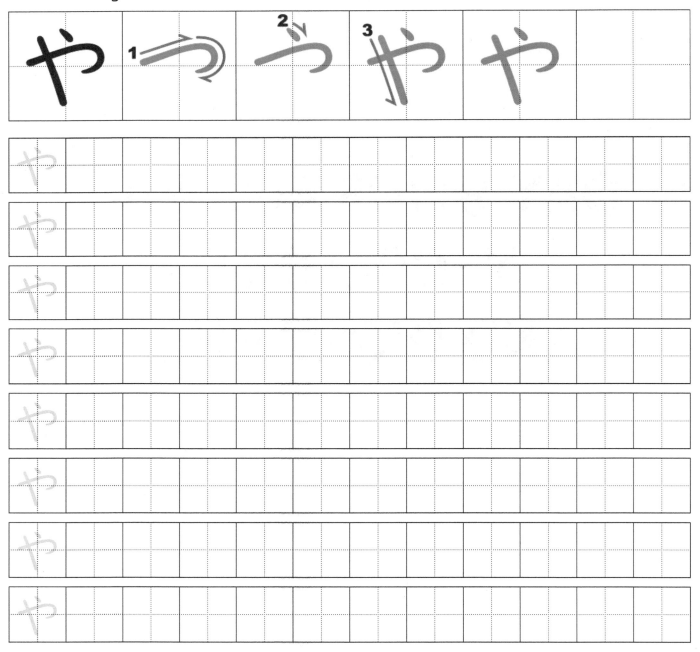

Try imagining this character as a <u>u</u>nicorn to better remember it.

[yu]

Practice writing this character:

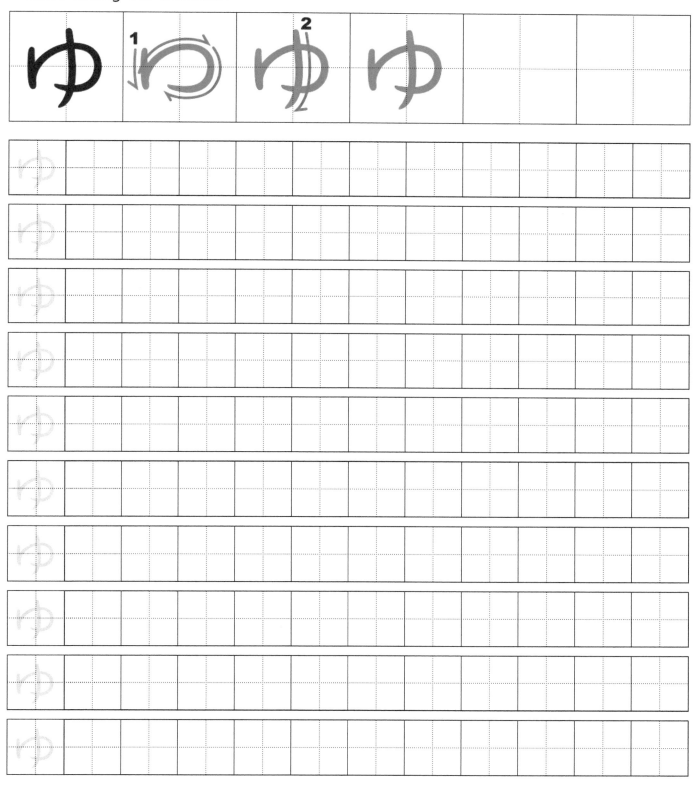

 **[yo]**

 Remember this character by imagining it as a <u>yo-yo</u> toy dangling from a finger.

Practice writing this character:

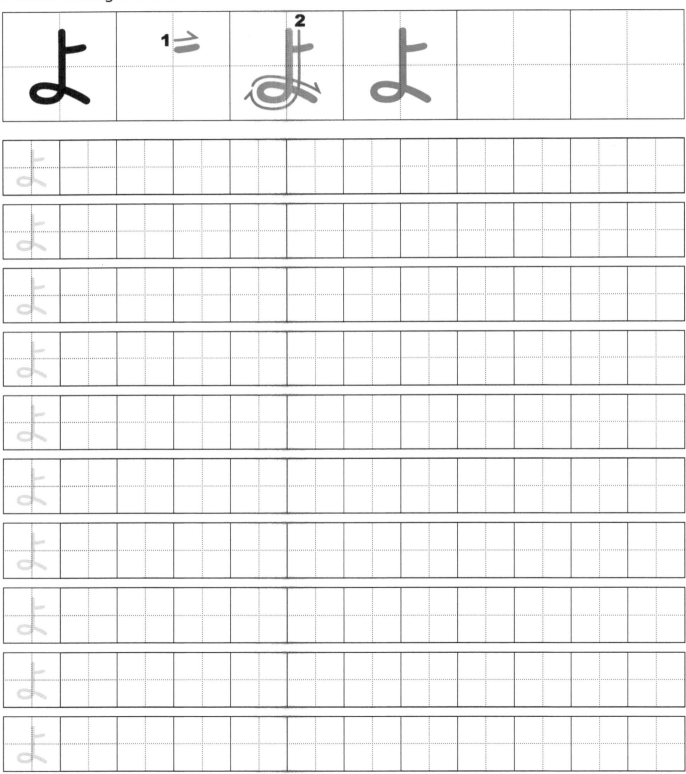

HIRAGANA DIGRAPHS

Characters や [ya], ゆ [yu], よ [yo] can be combined with [i] sound consonants to form digraphs or 'yoon'. In that case や [ya], ゆ [yu], よ [yo] are written smaller. Here are the hiragana digraphs:

りゃ	みゃ	ぴゃ	びゃ	ひゃ	にゃ	ちゃ	じゃ	しゃ	ぎゃ	きゃ
[rya]	[mya]	[pya]	[bya]	[hya]	[nya]	[cha]	[ja]	[sha]	[gya]	[kya]
りゅ	みゅ	ぴゅ	びゅ	ひゅ	にゅ	ちゅ	じゅ	しゅ	ぎゅ	きゅ
[ryu]	[myu]	[pyu]	[byu]	[hyu]	[nyu]	[chu]	[ju]	[shu]	[gyu]	[kyu]
りょ	みょ	ぴょ	びょ	ひょ	にょ	ちょ	じょ	しょ	ぎょ	きょ
[ryo]	[myo]	[pyo]	[byo]	[hyo]	[nyo]	[cho]	[jo]	[sho]	[gyo]	[kyo]

Technically you could form digraphs with ぢ as well but they are no longer in use.

Remember! When pronouncing the digraphs it is important to slide to the y-sound right after the consonant. Otherwise you may end up saying a completely different word. For example:

きょう   and   きよう

[kyou] - today   [kiyou] - skillful

りゅう   and   りゆう

[ryuu] - dragon   [riyuu] - reason

WORD WRITING PRACTICE

Let's revise the characters that we've learned and write some words with them!

にぎやか [nigiyaka] — lively, busy

にぎやか

はやい [hayai] — early or fast

はやい

へや [heya] — room

へや

やさい [yasai] — vegetable

やさい

いしゃ [isha] — doctor

いしゃ

おちゃ [ocha] — tea

おちゃ

かいしゃ [kaisha] — company, corporation

かいしゃ

じてんしゃ [jitensha] — bicycle

じてんしゃ

ちゃいろ [chairo] — brown

ちゃいろ

およぐ [oyogu] — to swim

およぐ

いっしょ [issho] — together

いっしょ

きょうしつ [kyoushitsu] — classroom

きょうしつ

じしょ [jisho] — dictionary

じしょ

じゅぎょう [jyugyou] — lesson

じゅぎょう

ぎゅうにく [gyuuniku] — beef

ぎゅうにく

ぎゅうにゅう [gyuunyuu] — milk

ぎゅうにゅう

ゆき [yuki] — snow

ゆき

しょうゆ [shoyu] — soy sauce

しょうゆ

ふゆ [fuyu] — winter

ふゆ

やま [yama] — mountain

やま

やおや [yaoya] — greengrocer

やおや

ほんやく [honyaku] — translation

ほんやく

はやし [hayashi] — grove

はやし

びょうき [byouki] — illness

びょうき

ひゃく [hyaku] — hundred

ひゃく

こうちゃ [koucha] — black tea

こうちゃ

しゃかい [shakai] — society

しゃかい

ゆび [yubi] — finger

ゆび

よい [yoi] — good

よい

わ、を、ん

DAY 10: HIRAGANA W-COLUMN AND 'N' CHARACTER

HIRAGANA W-COLUMN AND 'N' CHARACTER

わ [wa], を [wo], ん [n]

Today you'll learn 3 new characters and 2 new sounds.

 **[wa]**

 To remember this character imagine it as a <u>w</u>hite <u>s</u>wan floating on the <u>wa</u>ter.

Practice writing this character:

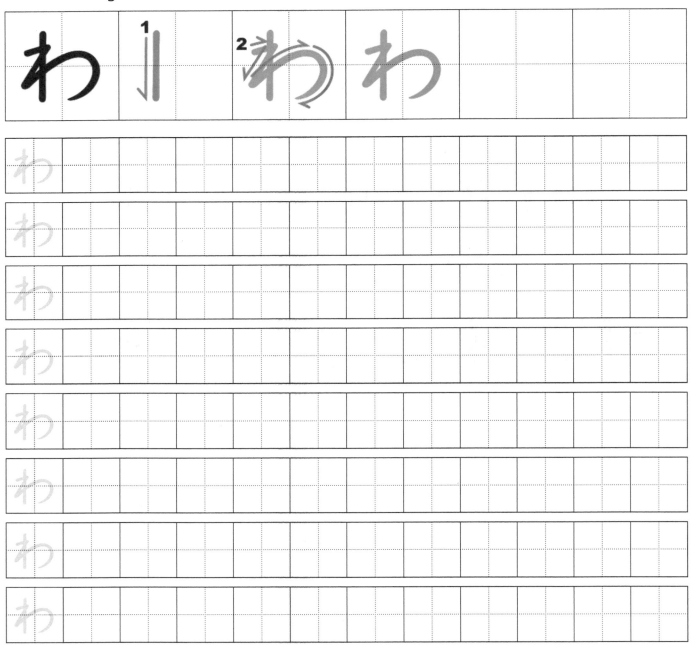

Imagine this character as crack in the <u>wall</u> to remember it better.

[wo/o]

Character を [wo] is never used in a word but only as an object marking particle. The word before を would be the object of the sentence. For example:

りんごをたべています。

[Ringo <u>o</u> tabete imasu.] - I am eating an apple.

Practice writing this character:

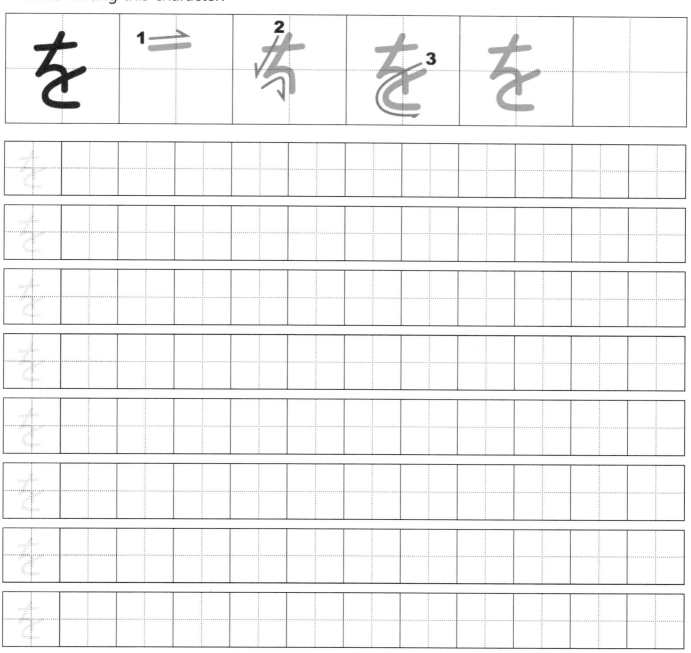

 **[n/m]**

 This character is easy to remember as it looks like an italicized 'n'.

Character ん [n] is rather special. You cannot start a word with it. It can only be found at the end or in the middle of a word.

Another thing to remember is that ん can sound different depending on the context. It is pronounced as [m] after b- and p-sounds and it can sound like [ng] if it comes before a g-sound. For example:

かんぱい
[kanpai] - Cheers
ん pronounced as [m]

はんがく
[hangaku] - writing
ん pronounced as [ng]

Practice writing this character:

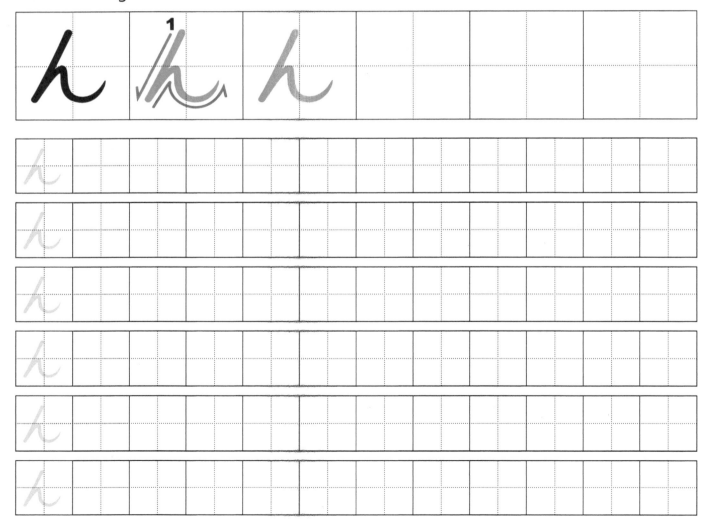

WORD WRITING PRACTICE

Let's revise the characters that we've learned and write some words with them!

うわぎ [uwagi] — coat, jacket

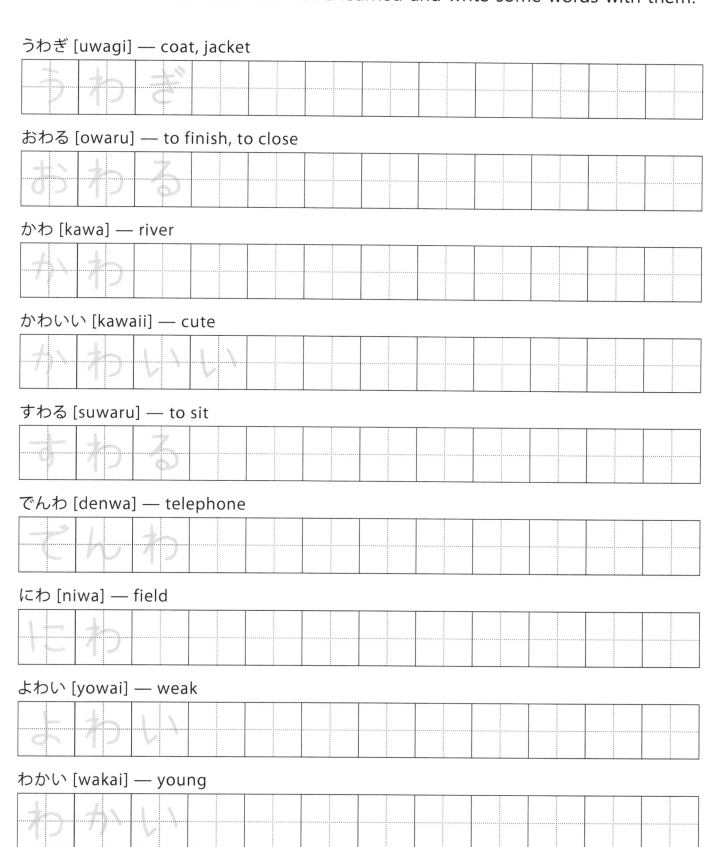

おわる [owaru] — to finish, to close

かわ [kawa] — river

かわいい [kawaii] — cute

すわる [suwaru] — to sit

でんわ [denwa] — telephone

にわ [niwa] — field

よわい [yowai] — weak

わかい [wakai] — young

わかる [wakaru] — to understand

わかる

わすれる [wasureru] — to forget

わすれる

わたし [watashi] — I, myself

わたし

わたす [watasu] — to pass over, to hand over

わたす

わたる [wataru] — to cross over, to go across

わたる

わるい [warui] — bad

わるい

あさごはん [asagohan] — breakfast

あさごはん

いちばん [ichiban] — best, first

いちばん

えいがかん [eigakan] — movie theater

えいがかん

おかあさん [okaasan] — (respectful) mother

おかあさん

おじいさん [ojiisan] — (respectful) grandfather

おとうさん [otousan] — (respectful) father

おばあさん [obaasan] — (respectful) grandmother

おんな [onna] — woman, girl

がいこくじん [gaikokujin] — foreigner

かんじ [kanji] — kanji, Chinese character

ぎんこう [ginkou] — bank

げんかん [genkan] — entrance

げんき [genki] — health

きんようび [kinyoubi] — Friday

でんしゃ [densha] — electric train

ごぜん [gozen] — morning, a.m.

じかん [jikan] — time

しんぶん [shinbun] — newspaper

たいしかん [taishikan] — embassy

たいへん [taihen] — very

たぶん [tabun] — perhaps, probably

たんじょうび [tanjoubi] — birthday

てんき [tenki] — weather

としょかん [toshokan] — library

フラッシュカード

HIRAGANA CUT-OUT FLASH CARDS

か	あ
き	い
く	う
け	え
こ	お

a	ka
i	ki
u	ku
e	ke
o	ko

た	さ
ち	し
つ	す
て	せ
と	そ

sa	ta
shi	chi
su	tsu
se	te
so	to

は	な
ひ	に
ふ	ぬ
へ	ね
ほ	の

na	ha
ni	hi
nu	fu
ne	he
no	ho

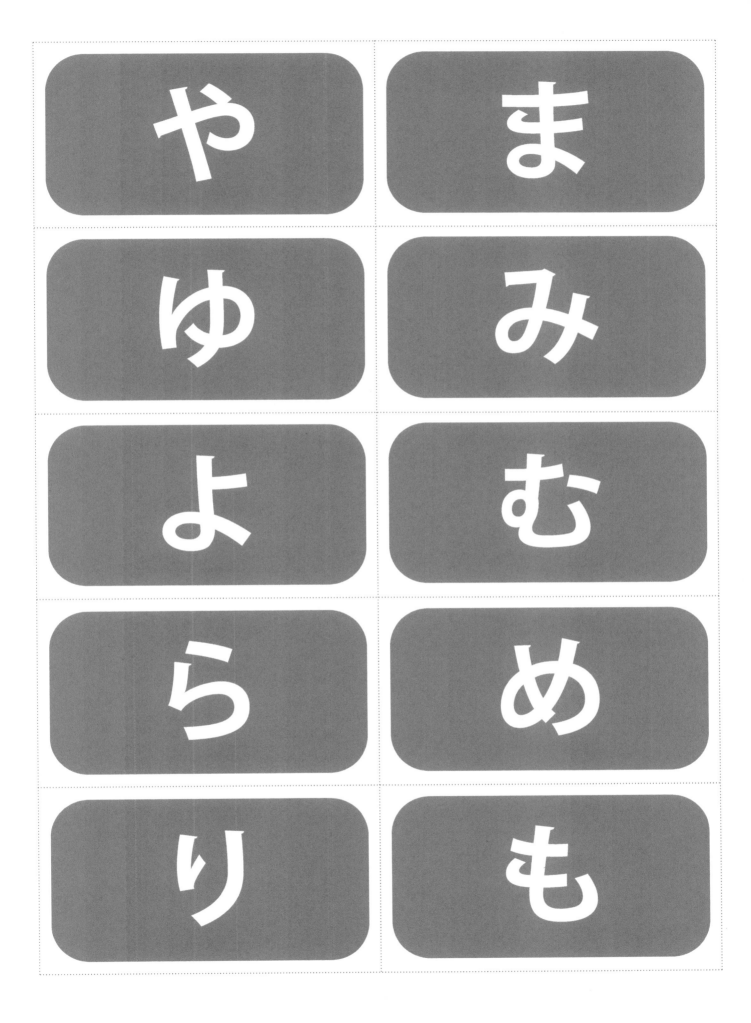

ma	ya
mi	yu
mu	yo
me	ra
mo	ri

ん	る
	れ
	ろ
	わ
	を

ru	n
re	
ro	
wa	
wo	

HIRAGANA CHART

あ a	か ka	さ sa	た ta	な na	は ha	ま ma	や ya	ら ra	わ wa
い i	き ki	し shi	ち chi	に ni	ひ hi	み mi		り ri	
う u	く ku	す su	つ tsu	ぬ nu	ふ fu	む mu	ゆ yu	る ru	
え e	け ke	せ se	て te	ね ne	へ he	め me		れ re	
お o	こ ko	そ so	と to	の no	ほ ho	も mo	よ yo	ろ ro	を wo

ん n